Table of contents

02 • Wonderful Tonight

04 • Against All Odds

05 • Can't Help Falling In Love

07 • You Raise Me Up

09 • Can't Take My Eyes Off Of You

10 • The Closest Thing To Crazy

12 • Mamma Mia

14 • I'll Stand By You

16 • Ring Of Fire

18 • Jingle Bell Rock

20 • Imagine

22 • Tears In Heaven

24 • Thriller

27 • Hello

28 • Titanium (feat. Sia)

30 • Thinking Out Loud

32 • Dancing Queen

33 • Yesterday

34 • We Are The Champions

35 • Unchained Melody

36 • We Are The World

37 • All You Need Is Love

38 • The Nearness Of You

39 • Danger Zone

40 • Viva La Vida

42 • Piano Man

43 • You Are So Beautiful

44 • Right Here Waiting

45 • The Lion Sleeps Tonight

46 • Billie Jean

48 • Smoke On The Water

49 • Hotel California

50 • No Woman No Cry

51 • Oh, Pretty Woman

53 • Amazing Grace

54 • Just The Two Of Us

55 • Hey Jude

57 • Perfect

58 • We Will Rock You

59 • Party In The U.S.A.

60 • Silent Night

62 • Schindler's List

64 • Top Gun (Anthem)

66 • Unforgettable

67 • Hallelujah

68 • Bohemian Rhapsody

70 • Yakety Sax

72 • Someone To Watch Over Me

75 • Precious Lord, Take My Hand

77 • Lean On Me

79 • Try A Little Tenderness

81 • (I've Had) The Time Of My Life

84 • I Got You (I Feel Good)

86 • Last Friday Night

88 • Firework

91 • Auld Lang Syne

92 • Sunny

93 • Let's Stay Together

94 • Here Comes The Sun

95 • When I'm Sixty-Four

96 • Old Time Rock & Roll

97 • Fly Me To The Moon

98 • Leaving On A Jet Plane

99 • Crazy

100 • Superstition

101 • Baker Street

101 • Peter Gunn

103 • Africa

Wonderful Tonight

Medium tempo

Words & Music by Eric Clapton

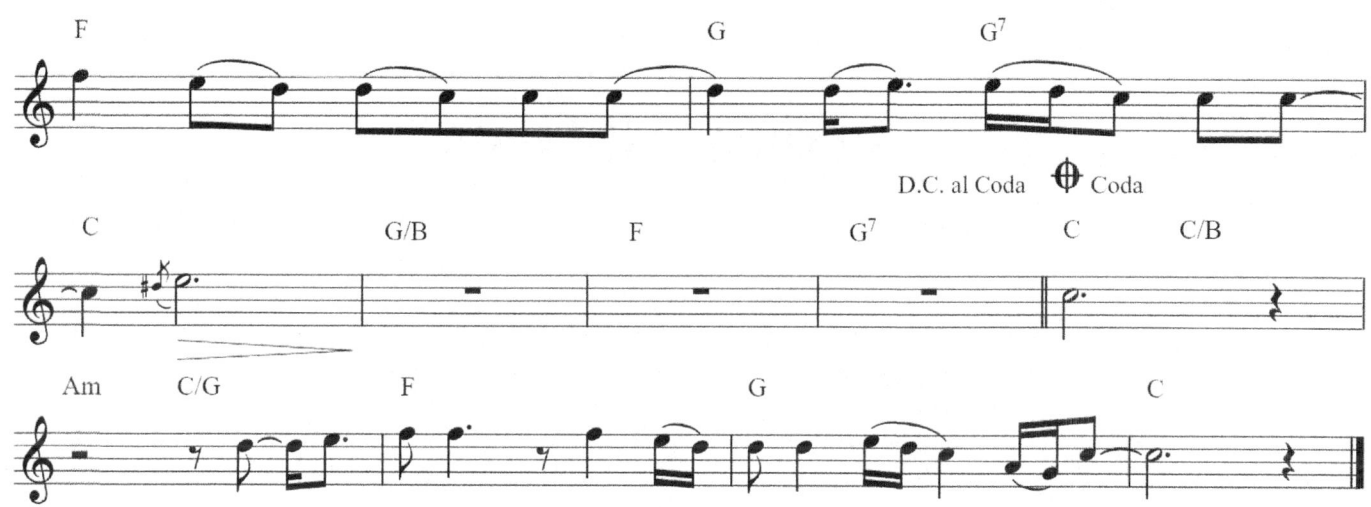

D.C. al Coda ⊕ Coda

Against All Odds

Can't Help Falling In Love

In a slow 50s style

Words & Music by George David
Weiss, Hugo Peretti & Luigi Creatore

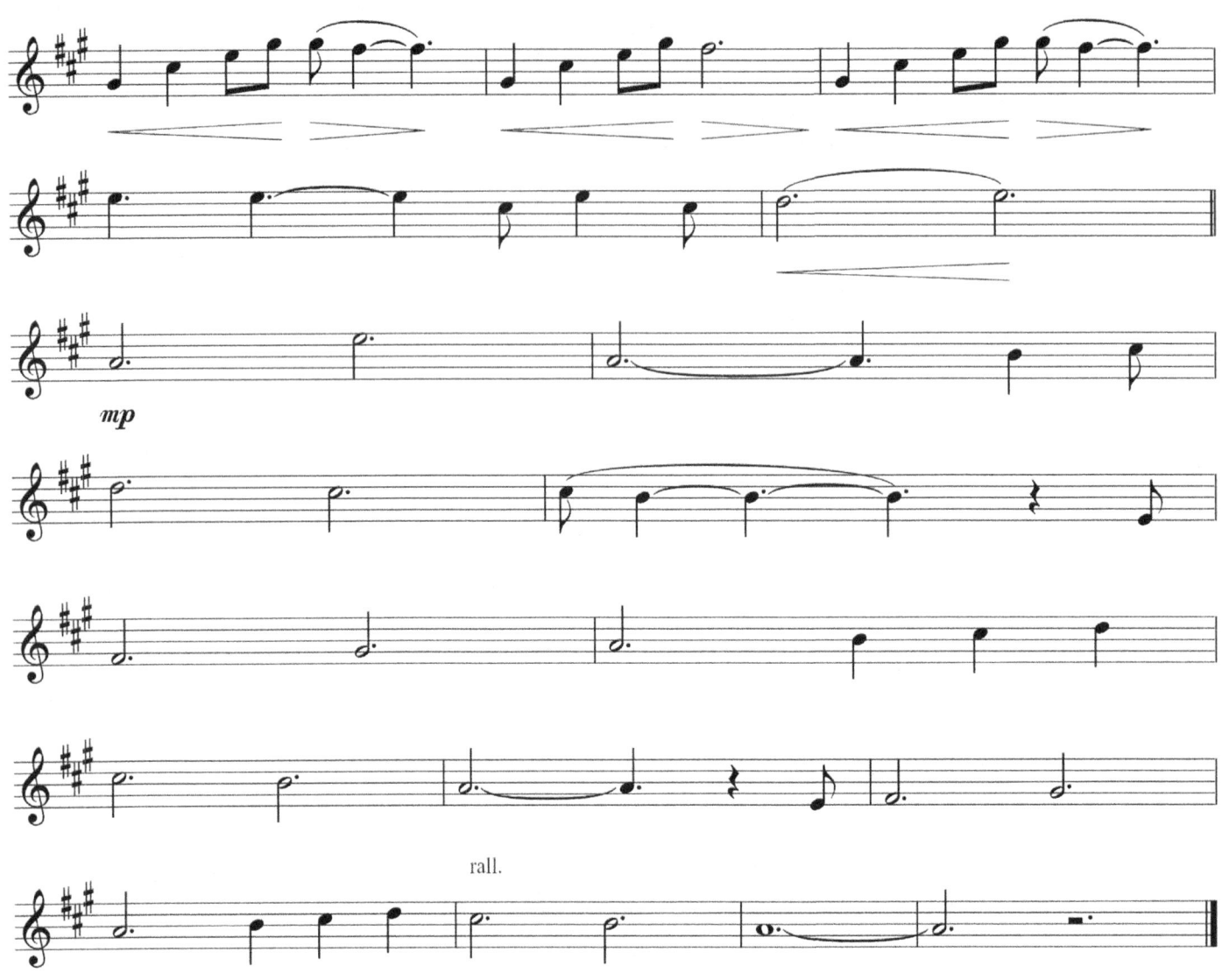

You Raise Me Up

Words & Music by George David Weiss,
Hugo Peretti & Luigi Creatore

Can't Take My Eyes Off Of You

The Four Seasons

The Closest Thing To Crazy

Gently

Words & Music by Mike Batt

Alto Saxophone

Mamma Mia

Words & Music by Benny Andersson,
Stig Anderson & Björn Ulvaeus

I'll Stand By You

Soulfully ♩ = 67

Words & Music by Chrissie Hynde, Tom Kelly & Billy Steinberg

Ring Of Fire

Upbeat Country ♩ = 104

Words & Music by Merle Kilgore & June Carter

trumpets cue

Repeat to fade

dim. poco a poco

17

Jingle Bell Rock

Words & Music by Joseph Beal & James Boothe

Imagine

Words & Music by John Lennon

Tears In Heaven

Words & Music by Eric Clapton & Will Jennings

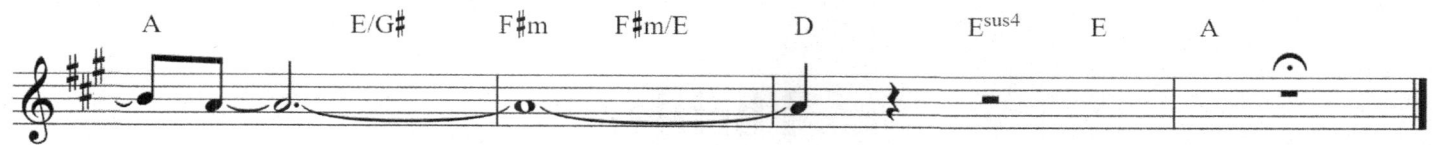

Thriller

Words & Music by Rod Temperton

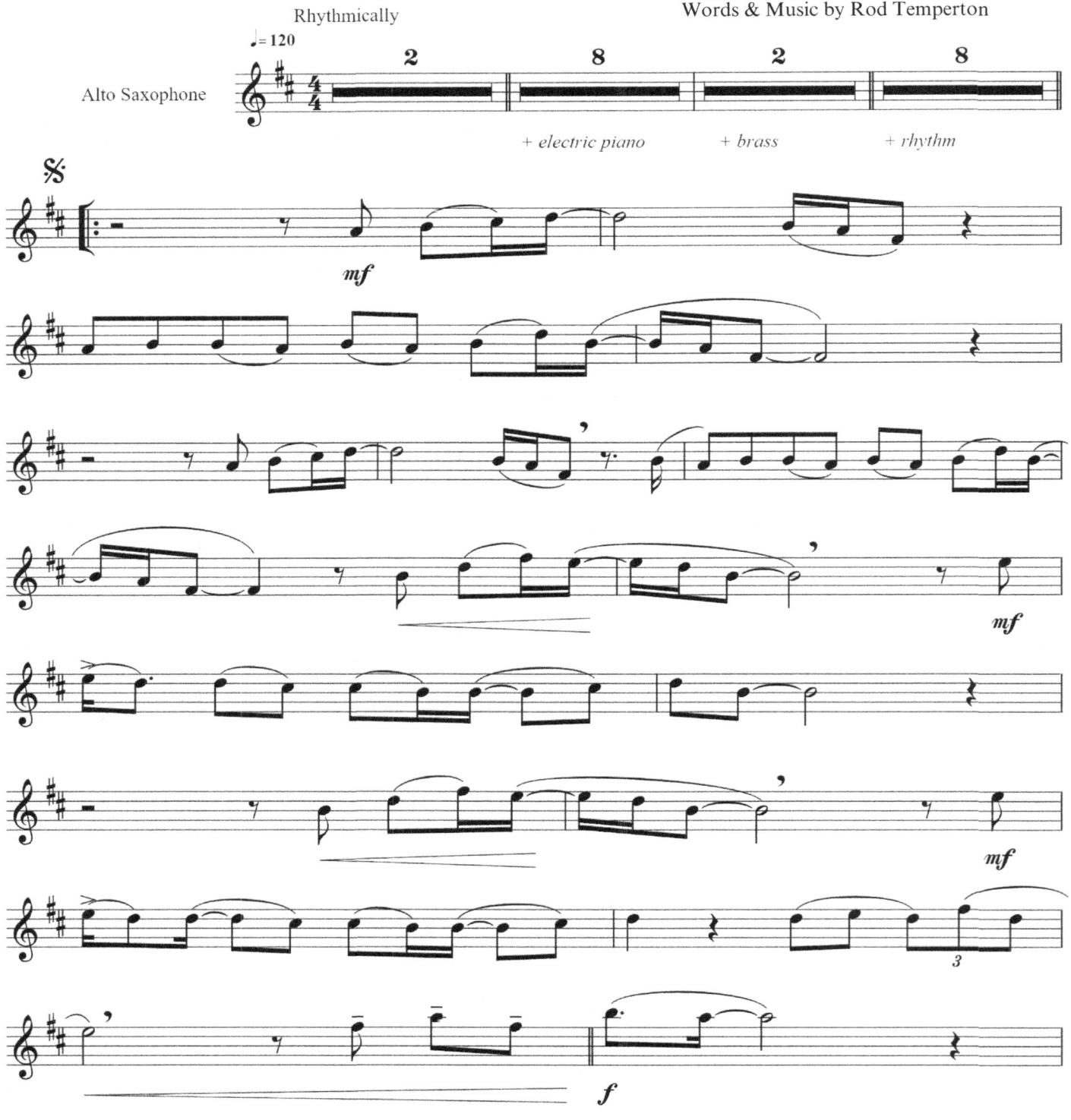

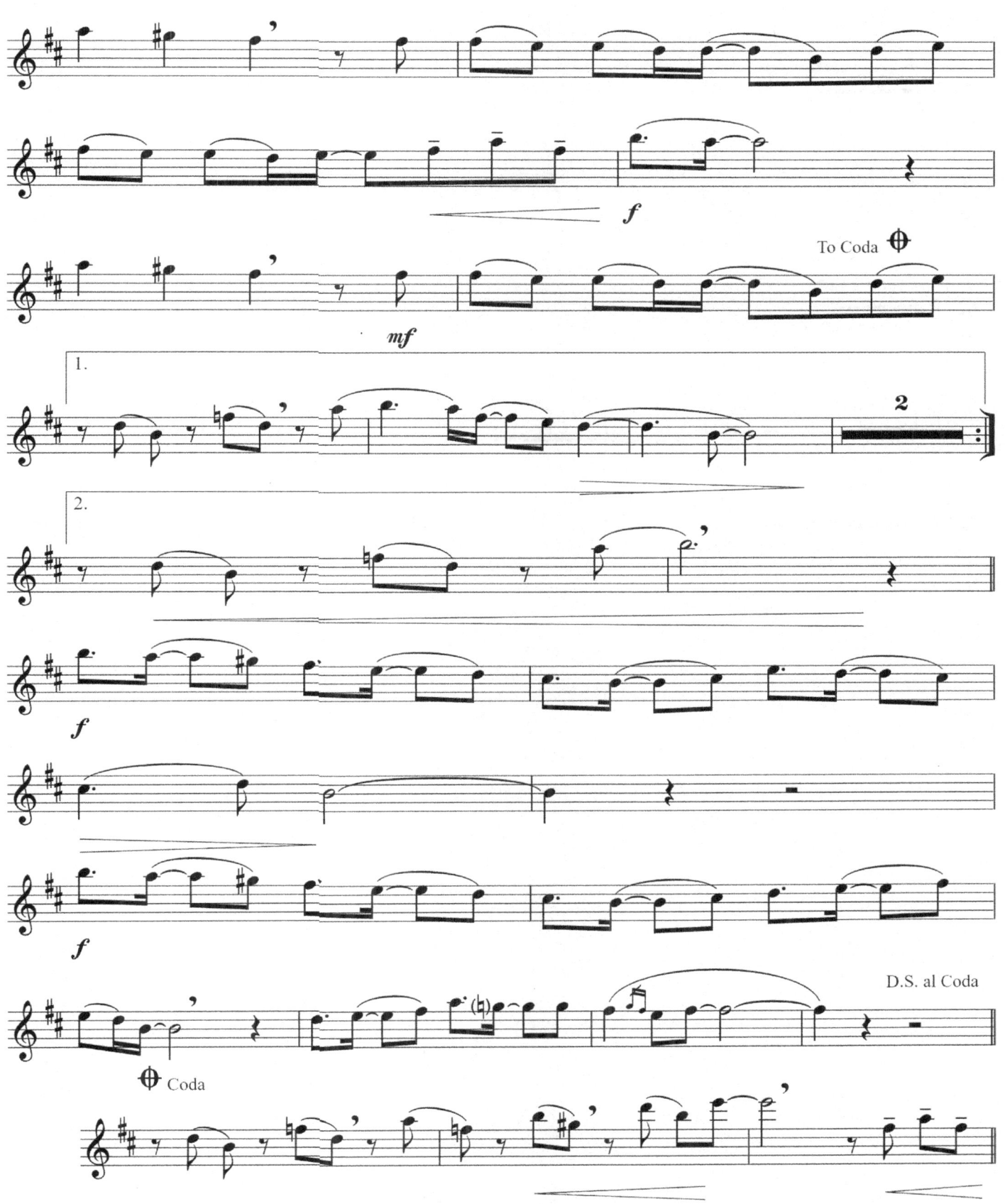

Hello

Words & Music by Lionel Richie

Titanium

Words & Music by Sia Furler, David Guetta,
Giorgio Tuinfort & Nick van de Wall

(2nd time cresc.)

Thinking Out Loud

Simply

Words & Music by Ed Sheeran & Amy Wadge

Dancing Queen

Words and Music by BENNY ANDERSSON,
BJORN ULVAEUS and STIG ANDERSON

Yesterday

Words and Music by JOHN LENNON
and PAUL McCARTNEY

We Are The Champions

Words and Music by
FREDDIE MERCURY

Unchained Melody

Lyric by HY ZARET
Music by ALEX NORTH

We Are The World

Words and Music by LIONEL RICHIE
and MICHAEL JACKSON

All You Need Is Love

Words and Music by JOHN LENNON
and PAUL McCARTNEY

The Nearness Of You

Words by NED WASHINGTON
Music by HOAGY CARMICHAEL

Danger Zone

Words and Music by GIORGIO MORODER
and TOM WHITLOCK

Viva La Vida

Words and Music by GUY BERRYMAN, JON
BUCKLAND, WILL CHAMPION and CHRIS MARTIN

40

Piano Man

Words and Music by
BILLY JOEL

You Are So Beautiful

Words and Music by BILLY PRESTON
and BRUCE FISHER

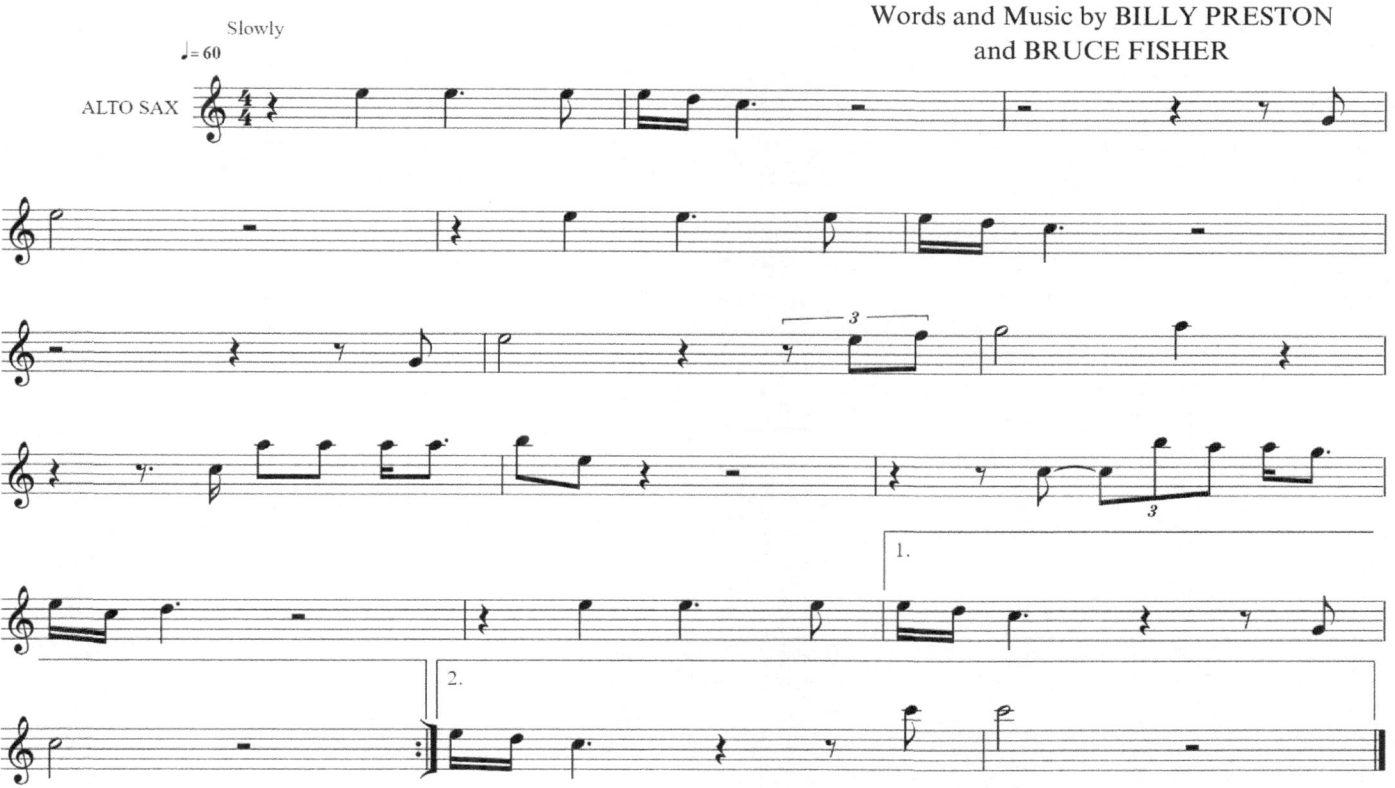

Right Here Waiting

Words and Music by RICHARD MARX

The Lion Sleeps Tonight

New Lyrics and Revised Music by GEORGE DAVID WEISS,
HUGO PERETTI and LUIGI CREATORE

Billie Jean

Words and Music by
MICHAEL JACKSON

Smoke On The Water

Words and Music by RITCHIE BLACKMORE,
IAN GILLAN, ROGER GLOVER,
JON LORD and IAN PAICE

Hotel California

Words and Music by DON HENLEY,
GLENN FREY and DON FELDER

No Woman No Cry

Words and Music by
VINCENT FORD

Oh, Pretty Woman

Words and Music by ROY ORBISON
and BILL DEES

Amazing Grace

Just The Two Of Us

Words and Music by RALPH MacDONALD,
WILLIAM SALTER and BILL WITHERS

Hey Jude

HEY Words and Music by JOHN LENNON
and PAUL McCARTNEY

Perfect

Words and Music by
ED SHEERAN

We Will Rock You

Words and Music by
BRIAN MAY

Party In The U.S.A.

Words and Music by JESSICA CORNISH,
LUKASZ GOTTWALD and CLAUDE KELLY

Silent Night

Peacefully ♩ = 76

Words by Joseph Mohr Music by Franz Gruber

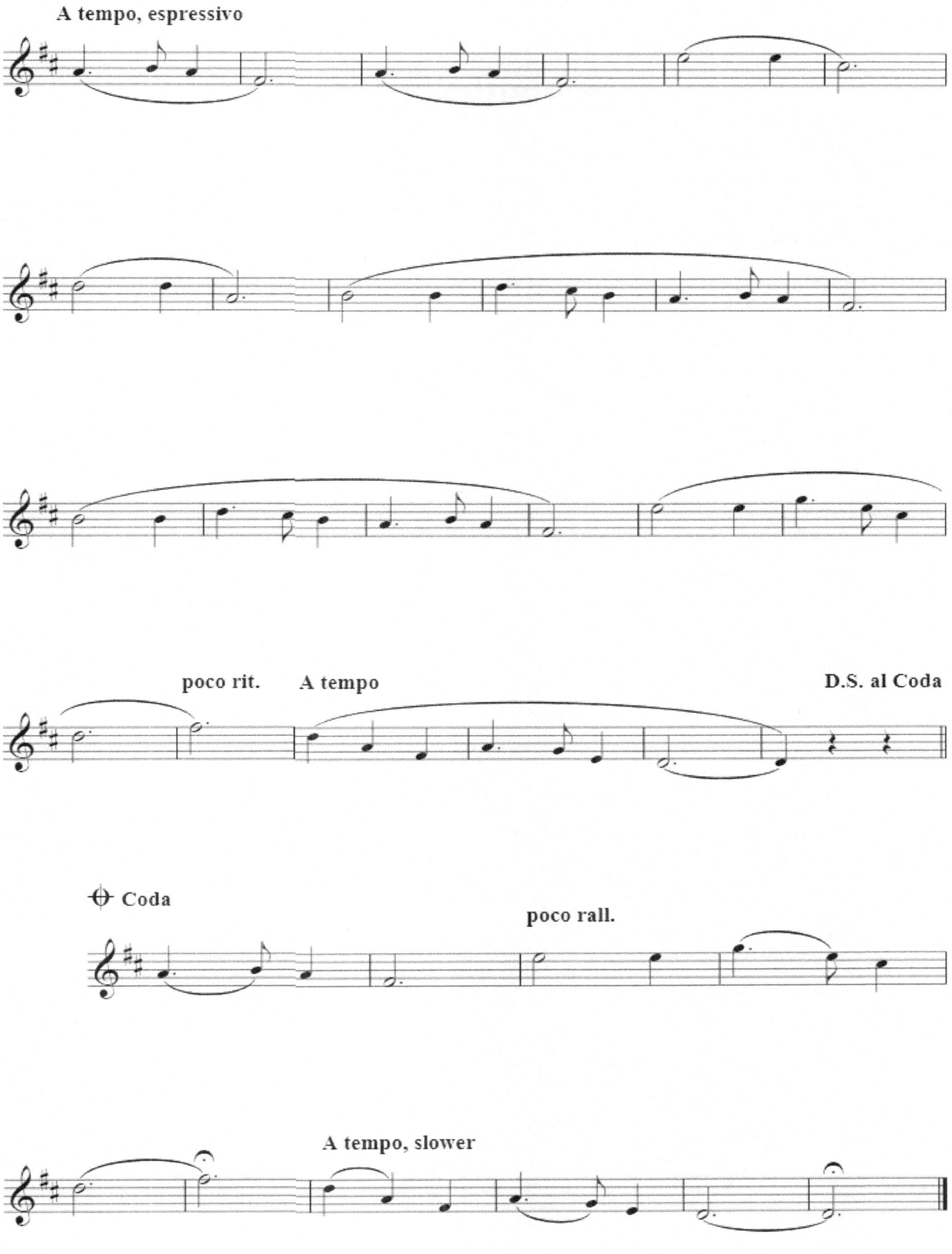

A tempo, espressivo

poco rit.　　A tempo

D.S. al Coda

Coda

poco rall.

A tempo, slower

Schindler's List

Composed by John William

Slowly ♩ = 50

mp *teneramente*

più mosso (♩ = 55)

mf

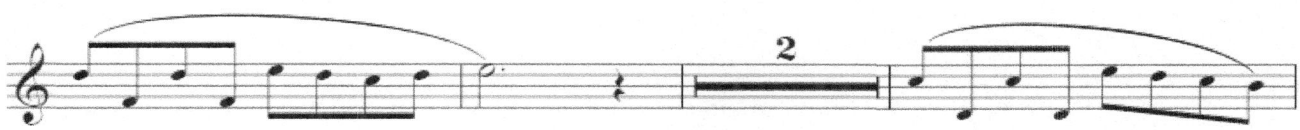

Top Gun (Anthem)

Unforgettable

Words and Music by
IRVING GORDON

Hallelujah

Words and Music by
LEONARD COHEN

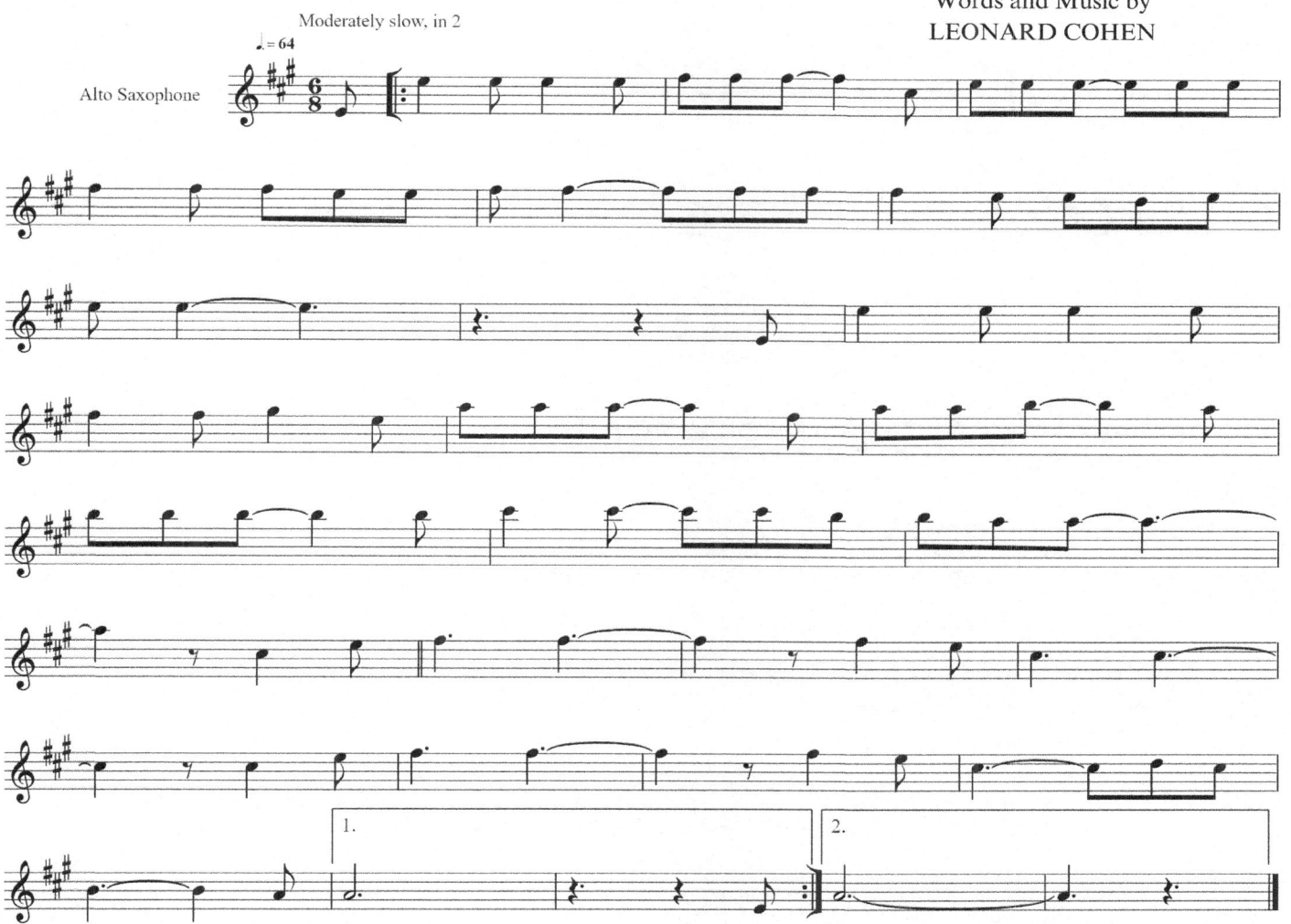

Bohemian Rhapsody

Words and Music by
FREDDIE MERCURY

Yakety Sax

Someone To Watch Over Me

Tenderly, straight quavers

Music by George Gershwin

cresc.

rit.

A tempo

p

mp

mf cantabile

mp

Precious Lord, Take My Hand

Slowly ♩. = 64

Words & Music by Thomas A.Dorsey

Slower

a tempo   rall.

2

Lean On Me

Relaxed and softly ♩ = 72

Lean On MeWords & Music by Bill Withers

f espressivo

mf

molto rit.

mp

p

78

Try A Little Tenderness

Words & Music by Harry Woods, Jimmy
Campbell & Reg Connelly

80

The Time Of My Life

Words & Music by Frankie Previte, John
DeNicola & Donald Markowitz

Moderately ♩ = 109

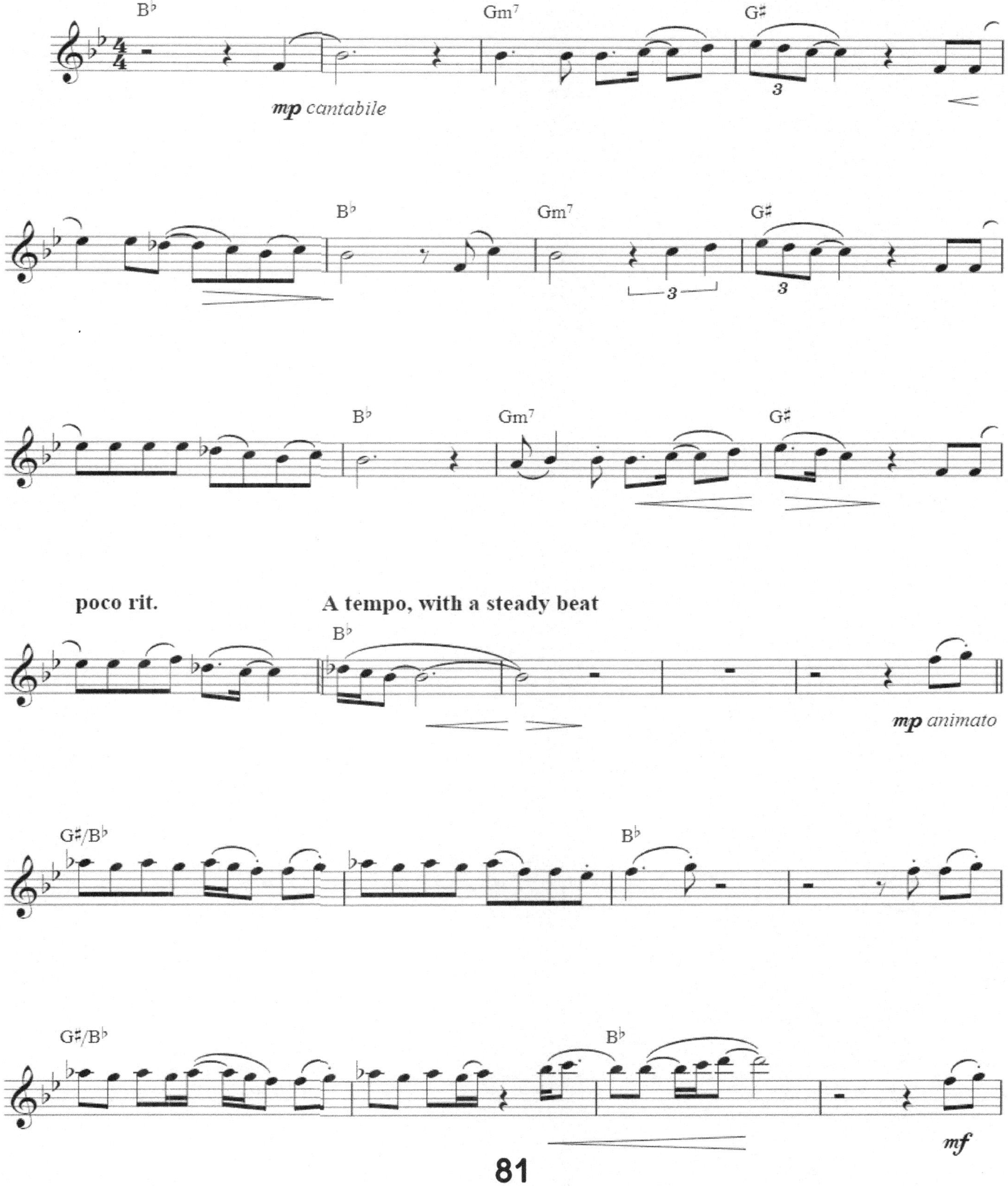

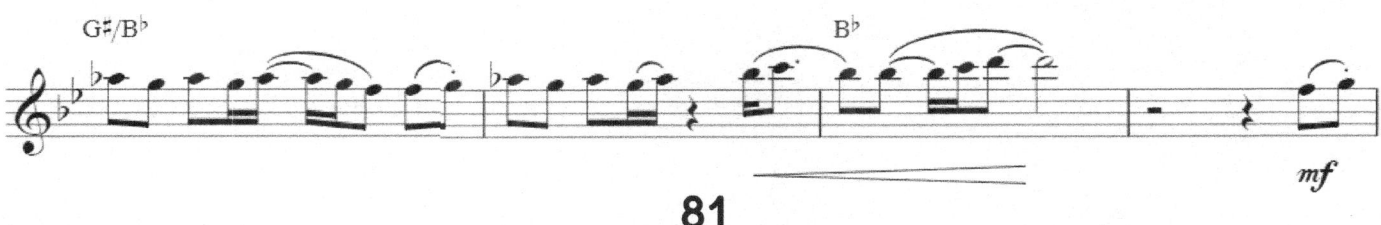

mp *animato*

cresc. poco a poco

D.S. al Coda   **⊕ Coda**

mf

83

I Got You

Words & Music by James Brown

Last Friday Night

Words & Music by Max Martin,
Lukasz Gottwald, Bonnie McKee & Katy Perry

87

Firework

Words & Music by Tor Erik Hermansen, Katy Perry,
Mikkel S. Eriksen, Sandy Wilhelm & Ester Dean

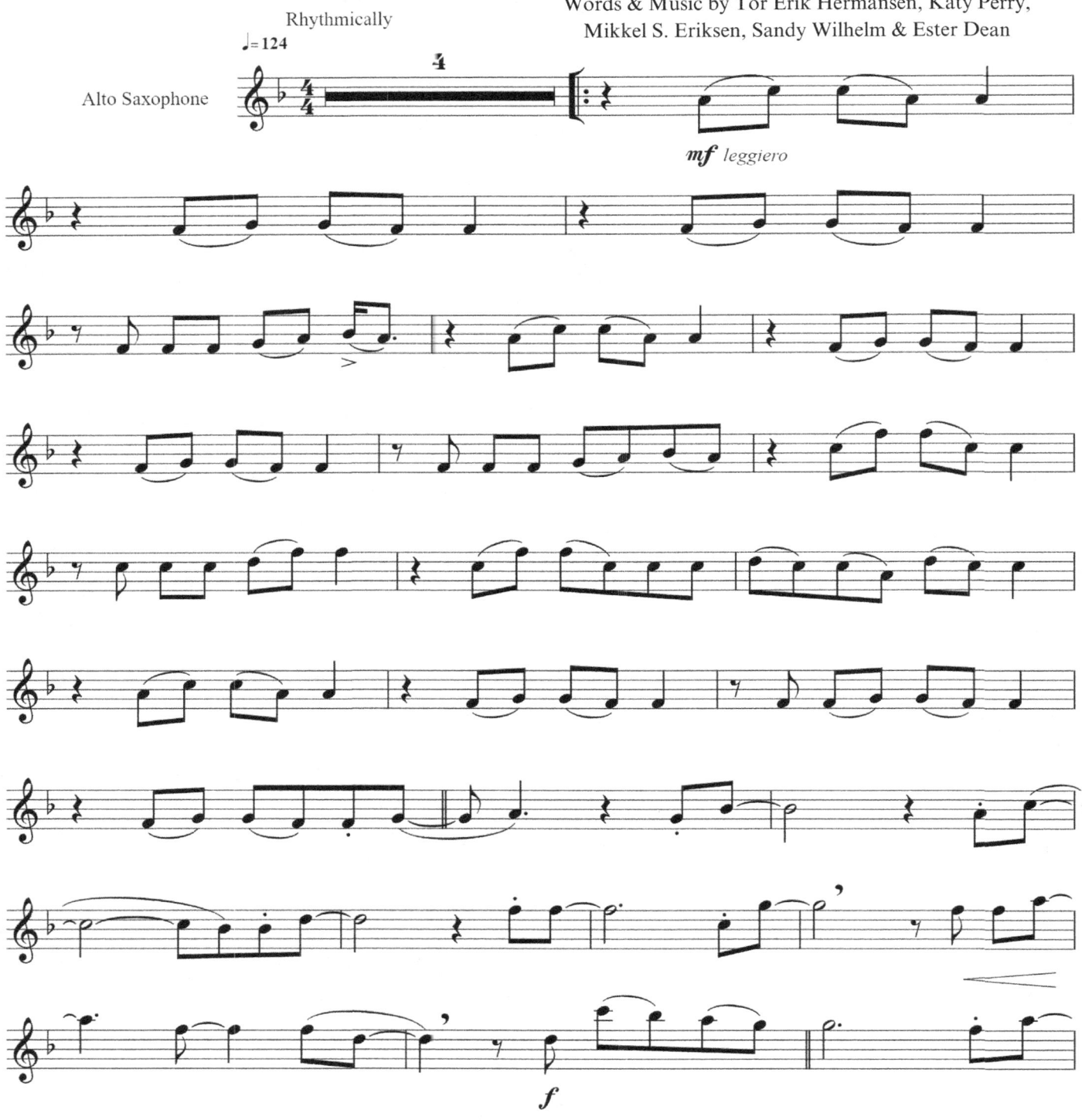

89

Auld Lang Syne

Sunny

Words and Music by
BOBBY HEBB

Let's Stay Together

Words and Music by AL GREEN,
WILLIE MITCHELL and AL JACKSON, JR.

Here Comes The Sun

Words and Music by
GEORGE HARRISON

When I'm Sixty-Four

Words and Music by JOHN LENNON
and PAUL McCARTNEY

Old Time Rock & Roll

Words and Music by GEORGE JACKSON
and THOMAS E. JONES III

Fly Me To The Moon

Words and Music by
BART HOWARD

Leaving On A Jet Plane

Words and Music by
JOHN DENVER

Crazy

Words and Music by
WILLIE NELSON

Superstition

Baker Street

Words and Music by
GERRY RAFFERTY

Peter Gunn

By HENRY MANCINI

Africa

Words and Music by DAVID PAICH
and JEFF PORCARO

Play 3 times

To Coda

Made in the USA
Coppell, TX
10 September 2023